Lead Generate or Die!

DR. TAMEKA BRYANT

DEDICATION

This book is dedicated to all of entrepreneurs that find a way to make it work!

CONTENTS

Acknowledgments

ABOUT THE BOOK

This book is a compilation of lead generation tools and ideas from 9 authors. As a business owner that continuously finds creative ways to capture leads, I thought it would be a great idea to compile a book.

If you are in the business of identifying new business and do so by generating leads, this is the book for you. We hope you enjoy each author's take on the area/s of expertise.

Happy Reading!

Chapter 1
Tameka Bryant

Dr. Tameka Bryant
Be-Niched.com

Describe your business.

As of this writing, I'm currently a real estate broker. As vague as that sounds and is, it's what I do most of the day. I broker deals and provide management and oversight for real estate agents. Most of my other time is spent coaching, writing courses and bringing relevant, ready-to-use resources to real estate agents and businesses so they can increase their bottom lines.

What unique ways do you use to obtain leads?

I gain leads in a variety of ways, but the one that I use to generate 100 leads a day is my surveys on social media. These are unique because they are free to create, easy to use and each one is created with the end user in mind. So, no two are the same. And this technique is free! No out of pocket expenses.

There are other ways I gain leads that may not be unique to some; I just put a spin on them. One in particular is through strategic networking. Attending networking events is a way for me to connect personally to a targeted group. I scout events that fit my client profile. I then work to find out which of my colleagues are attending and who the guest list includes. Once I have an idea of who may be there, I check to see if any of my colleagues can make an introduction. I have my ask prepared, then I make sure to not spend more than 10 minutes talking to my new connection. At the end of each conversation, I make sure I have exchanged cards and if possible set up an appointment to meet again in the near future. Then I proceed to working the event to reach the number of new contacts I had previously set out to connect with. I ALWAYS go out knowing how many new connections I want to make.

When did you get into the business?

I got in to the real estate business in 1990 as I was scouting my first piece of real estate in New York. I became an investor in 1997, a licensed real estate agent in 2002 and a licensed broker in 2004. In 2007, I became a licensed instructor. As with anything I do, it's an ongoing learning and growing experience so each year I "get into" the business a little deeper and learn something new.

What is your WHY?

My WHY is my family. I love being able to have a career that allows me to create a lifestyle that we all can enjoy. My children, now 19 and 23, grew up in the business. And since most of what I did I could do from home, I was still able to be near them all the time. We have traveled together, worked on homes (rehabbing), attended conferences and so much more as a team in building our business. Knowing that what I'm teaching them will be invaluable to them and their children is why I do what I do. I'm building Generational Wealth.

What do you do better than your competition?

I don't believe I have any competitors. I know that's a weird thing to say and believe, but when I look around, I don't see anyone who is doing what I do. Mostly, I don't operate in a box the way I see other real estate agents and brokers do. I'm a creative being, so I look in the market, see what's missing and create it.

How many transactions have you completed so far?

2,108

What is your volume vs. your # of transactions so far?

I no longer sell individual homes. I retired from that on December 31, 2016! I am currently helping others with their businesses and selling packages and off-market properties to investors.

Think about the hardest thing you faced in business. How did or do you survive or get through tough times?

The year was 2004. I was laid off from my six-figure job on March 23. This job wasn't real estate related, but it was my 3rd advancement within the nonprofit industry within the last 5 years, so I was all pumped about the new gig. On that day, which is also my son's birthday, I thought I died. It was 9 a.m. and I was invited into the office, then it happened. "You're fired." For an hour, I was stuck because as much of a planner as I thought I was, I hadn't planned for this, or for the next blow. 10 a.m. … "I was just fired," said my husband. Yep! Both incomes lost on the same day, within the same hour. I sat in that office knowing that I did not have a backup plan. My normal safety zones were all gone. My mom was riddled with cancer and deep in my heart I knew her time was closer than the doctors stated. I was right, she died a few months later. So with a dad deceased 7 years prior and grandparents who died within the last 5 years, I was simply distraught.

After a month of licking my wounds, I had to come up with something. I knew real estate was something I wanted to do full time once I retired. I just didn't realize I needed to start that plan immediately. So on May 15, 2004, I began my own real estate firm. With a limited circle of influence, I reached from within and pulled on those transferable skills I utilized in my last job.

I did everything! I wrote grants, and used that skill to obtain a façade grant and commercial loan to purchase my first building. I became a Certified Minority Business. I used this to obtain a state contract to house water testers and to obtain a foreclosure management contract. I networked to build a Circle of Influence. I originated commercial loans. I volunteered at my Realtor association. I built a team from my dining room and we started shaking things up in the city. My initial team was my simply my husband and two little kids and then we grew. Yes, things were tough. But it taught me a lot. I know now that experiencing ALL that I went through meant I could endure anything.

I pushed through it by leaning on my faith. I never gave up. I mean I wanted to! I even contemplated suicide. Yes, it got that dark at times. I suffered in silence, but I reached from within and refused to give up. Glad I didn't, too! If I had, I'd never have known the feeling of being named Realtor of the Year, first African American MLS president or being in the top 1% of sales in a market I wasn't from.

What would you tell young or new agents?

The first thing I would tell young or new agents is to "Don't Get Caught in the Hype". There are simply way too many companies to choose from, but don't go with the one that had the best recruiters. Choose your niche first then shop for the company that can best support your goals. Here's why: Let's say you choose company A to place your license with. And a year later you decide you want to do commercial transactions or property management. There's a good chance the company you chose BEFORE you knew what you really wanted to do doesn't allow its agents to handle those transactions. So then you are left with leaving said brokerage or handing over the transaction to someone else instead of learning how to work the transaction. Don't you just hate when someone says "You need experience to work that area?" Well, how do I gain experience if I'm not allowed to work the deal? This just burns me up, because using a mentor for new transactions is the way to go, not just saying "no."

Secondly, I'd want new agents to know where the REAL money is in the business. If many of them knew, they wouldn't spend so much time playing someone else's game. In fact, some may find that their niche to riches may not call for a real estate license at all.

Pick up your copy of the book on Amazon or borrow a copy.

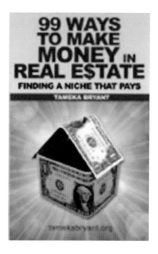

To connect with me, visit my site at www.be-niched.com.

Chapter 2
Jessica Hensley

Jessica Hensley
Owner of Heritage Homes

Describe your business.

I am the Broker/Owner of two small real estate offices in Southeast Kansas. There are 8 Agents who have their license with my company and we employ two transactions coordinators, one stager and one professional photographer. We specialize in residential & rural real estate, but we do handle the occasional commercial property. We opened in January 2015 and in 2016 we were the second ranking office in our MLS. My office is run much the same way as a mega agent running a team. I share all of my leads with my agents and provide staff for them to utilize, so that they can spend the majority of their time on activities that make money (writing contracts, showing houses, listing homes).

With my team, I was able to be the number one residential agent in 2015 and 2016 in our MLS. Going forward, my focus will be on building my company and my agents.

What unique ways do you use to obtain leads?

Social media is my mainstay for lead generation. I also have found a way to capture leads through building landing pages. Then I go back to social media with ads which provide others the opportunity to opt-in. I use Zillow, Realtor.com and Homes.com to lead generate as well.

I utilize contests through my FB page and award prizes to winners. These contests garner hundreds of comments and responses. Additionally, each time I have an open house, I will do a FB Live video, which produces a lot of interest and feedback. To further engage my audience, I host customer appreciation parties. Due to the success I am enjoying, I am working on a training program which helps agents utilize and maximize the Facebook platform to grow their businesses.

When did you get into business?

I happened on real estate. It was not intentional for me. My dad enrolled in a class in Oklahoma City. He paid for it but could not attend due to some unexpected change. He asked me take the class I had always been good at sales. I was the youngest attendee in the class. I passed the test and found a broker to work with and did so for 2 years. Then, I moved to Coffeyville and worked for another broker for 10 years until he passed away. At that point, my husband and I decided we didn't like our choices and thought we should open an office of our own. Up until that point, I was part-time in real estate as I also held other jobs working at a bank and as a financial advisor. I even received my insurance license during that 10-year period. I was averaging in real estate sales $250k -$1 million. I was not successful. I considered myself a failure in the business until 2014. I had a mental shift. That's when I decided "I am the owner, I am in charge of my business and that it falls on me whether it succeeds or not." Within three months of researching and figuring out the most innovative and latest ways to reach people and standout from my competition, it all turned around. Over the last two years, I have accelerated from the bottom of the barrel to the number one agent in my market.

What is your WHY for launching your business?

My WHY has evolved and changed over the years for sure. Initially, my why was to have a job. It was fun. Real estate was an easy career to get into without having a degree. My WHY today is to build a business that makes a difference in the lives of others and to be able to build my agents. I have eight agents I manage and four who are specifically on my team, and so I provide leads that assist in meeting their goals. The ability to have something that I can pass on to my son one day is where my WHY is now. My focus has changed from being money-driven to now trying to be a blessing.

What is the thing that motivates you? What drives you?

What keeps me going is the desire to achieve the greatest potential of my company. We want to be the premier business for people in this area. We want to be number one not because of money but because of the service we provide. We are an ethical company. We are currently not number one, but that's the next goal. It is rewarding to help my agents achieve their goals and that is something that motivates and drives me to do better.

What is your daily regimen that helps produce or maximize the results you are seeking?

I am always listening to something motivational. Whether it is a YouTube video, podcast, or daily meditation, it is something positive from others who have succeeded. I have to bring something positive into my heart and mind that allows me to get past the rough times in business and also gives me nuggets to share with my team.

What do you do better than your competition?

Besides the mentality shift, Facebook allowed me to do what my competitors were too afraid to do. What I do better than my competition is social media. Today's Realtor has an opportunity to reach thousands of people every day if you're willing to put yourself out there. You can build a massive audience in a small amount of time. You get people to like you and you can dominate your market.

How many transactions have you completed so far?

I have a lifetime sales completion of $27,455,189 and 325 transactions.

Think about the hardest thing you faced in business. How did or do you survive tough times?

I was seeking my Broker's license in Kansas. There are so many points needed to get the license, and I fell below the required number. So, I actually started applying in September 2014 and I did not actually get my Broker's license until June 2015. I opened my company in January 2015 so I hired another broker for my business until I achieved my own license. I applied three times for my license and was denied twice. It felt like a battle. It was frustrating. On my third application, I made an appearance before the KS Board, and they finally said yes. I told the board that if they said no now, I would continue to apply until they I received ayes.

What would you tell your younger self?

The first thing I would have told myself is budget your money a little bit better. Be more consistent with your time. Put in the work. Had I been as dedicated as I am now, then I would have been further along in my success.

What would you tell young or new agents?

New agents get discouraged really easily. They take things very personally. You must be able to separate yourself from the problem. Your job is to be a problem solver. You must look for solutions. It's not the time to throw up your hands and determine that it won't work. Remember, that it's not personal, it's business. You must recognize that you're not perfect. Admit your mistakes and learn from them. You're going to learn something from each transaction and correct it for next time.

Chapter 3
Trisha Alton

Trisha Alton
Trisha P. Realty Group

Describe your business.

We are a real estate team consisting of 12 licensed agents throughout all of Kansas City KS & MO, and surrounding areas. Two are assistants; one is our transaction coordinator and marketing guru, and the other also handles transaction coordination and runs our property management company. Our first hire was on September 1, 2015. After I realized I could not properly keep up on my own, I knew I needed to get an assist and a buyer's agent. My husband quit his government job to help me in the office and we hired a new agent in the business to help take on buyer leads. Since then, we have grown our team to what it is today.

What unique ways do you use to obtain leads?

We do many lead generations. Facebook is huge for us. We are also starting to tap into other social media platforms. We do purchase leads from Realtor.com, we also are a part of a few referral programs that have been very successful. We do "just sold" mailings, farming mailings, monthly newsletters, open houses and we are involved in our local Chamber of Commerce and Young Professional organizations. Our property management company also brings in leads.

When did you get into business?

I got into the business in February 2005, at the young age of 24! I was just finishing up college and was a bartender at the KCI Airport at the time.

What is your WHY? Why did you get into the business?

I was just finishing up college and my best friend from high school mentioned she was getting into real estate.   I had just purchased a home, but didn't think of it as something I was interested in. Well at that young age you do what your friends are doing, and the thought of hanging out with her every day sounded like a blast. So, I went ahead and got my license.

What is the thing that motivates you? What drives you?

A life of financial freedom motivates me. Setting up a life for my daughter where she will never have to struggle. I want to be able to go to the store and not worry if the money is there. I want my parents to be proud of the woman they raised, and I want to give my daughter someone to look up to. I want her to see that hard work does pay off.

What is your daily regimen that helps produce or maximize results you are seeking?

The first thing I do when I wake up is check Facebook and email and respond to any messages that came in overnight. I want people to have a message from me waiting before they wake up or get to the office. I check in with my real estate team most mornings through our Facebook messenger. I send them updates or motivational posts to get them ready for their day. The rest of the day I spend checking in with both assistants and following up with agents to see if they need help with anything. I contact my current clients and lenders to ensure my transactions are moving along smoothly. I then start working on prospecting for new leads. Daily cultivation is a must for new business.

What do you do better than your competition?

I hustle every day. I get out there so people see me. I have hired this team so that I had help when I was too busy. I don't try to do everything on my own. One person cannot be solely successful; it takes a team to build large wealth while still having a personal life. The property management company is a huge success for our business also, and most agents don't run both. I also firmly believe it takes money to make money. I will spend my money to make deals happen if the buyer/seller can't afford repairs or treatments. I would rather make a little than none. I am honest, whether you like it or not. I will point out all the bad things of a home so a buyer is in love with the home, not the decorations.

How many transactions have you completed so far?

In 2015, solely without my team, I sold 102 homes. In 2016, while building a team of 12 and still running my other businesses, I still personally sold 71 homes. In my career, I would guess that I have completed 500 transactions.

What is your volume vs. your # of transactions so far?

As a team in our first year, we end 2016 with $24,000,000 in sales and 167 units. I am very happy with or results and have high hopes for 2017.

Think about the hardest thing you faced in business. How did or do you survive or get through tough times?

The hardest thing I had to face was switching companies during busy season and my busiest year, which was 2015. The company I worked for was not pleased and did not make the move easy at all. It brought me down for a few weeks, but I got up and used my feelings to fuel my motivation. The switch in companies was the best decision I could have made, and I knew it would pay off soon. And it did!

Chapter 4
James Like

James Like
Revolution Real Estate

Describe your business.

Revolution Real Estate is a full service brokerage. We assist buyers and sellers as well as property management services through our sister company, Sonder Property Management. I founded the company in 2012 after 6 years in the real estate sales business. We are currently at 10 team members and $15 million in sales in 2016. We are shooting for $34 million in 2017.

What unique ways do you use to obtain leads?

90% of my business comes from referrals. Although that doesn't sound unique, most of those referrals are generated through social media and community involvement. Facebook has been the source of more than $10 million in business over the past 3 years. When you strive to bring value to people in their lives or businesses, you don't have to ask for business, it will naturally come your way. What does bringing value look like? It is making a call to a business owner in your database, asking them their goals, and seeing how you can bring them value or referrals. We consult small businesses, we do social media interviews with local businesses, we work with clients on goal setting and advice, etc. Doing this is invaluable, and you don't have to worry about getting the "I don't want people to feel used" feeling a lot of agents get.

When did you get into business?

January 2006 I started as an agent. I have been an investor since 2000.

What is your WHY? Why did you get into the business?

I got into the business to build something which had no ceiling for income and which could provide freedom in time and multiple streams of income. My Why really is Quality of Life. Doing something I love to do while having the best quality of life now and even better quality of life in the future for my family. My personal goal is to own 40 doors by 45 years of age. (I am 38 and have nine doors currently). I will retire and fulfill the dream of building microbusinesses for missionaries around the world.

What is the thing that motivates you? What drives you?

Believe it or not, money is not my motivating factor. Building a business and doing it with integrity while assisting people with possibly their biggest investment is the most rewarding part, along with adding more and more investment properties to my portfolio. Also, I am set on providing my family with the best life experience as we raise our three daughters. Travel is a passion for us as well. The more business and the bigger the team we build, the more we can travel and be flexible.

What is your daily regimen that helps produce or maximize results you are seeking?

Every day I try to engage with no less than six people. These people are in my community (database), social media, or face to face. I am always striving to offer them value while making myself known in the part of the brain called the reticular activator, so when they think real estate they think about me.

What do you do better than your competition?

I connect quickly with people. I can build rapport with many personalities, in person or on the phone, very fast.
How many transactions have you completed so far?
I have completed more than 300 transactions in 10 years, and most were done over the past three years.

What is your volume vs. number of transactions so far?

Roughly $50 million (average is about $150k per transaction currently)

Think about the hardest thing you faced in business. How did or do you survive or get through tough times?

In 2007 through 2011, the market and economy both tanked. The real estate market also had a drastic shift. It was my first shift to experience. I ended up relying on my other streams of income (property mgmt., BPOs, investments) to make it through. I also had to shift to a different clientele. Investors were the new hot thing. So I partnered with them. Overall, during tough times I rely on my faith, I try to roll with what the market offers and learn to adapt, and make sure during the good times I have put ample amounts of money in savings for the downtimes.

What would you tell your younger self?

Younger self, "Make sure you have sales, structure, systems, and staff." If you do this you will accomplish anything in business. But the greater of these is sales." It has taken me seven solid years to finally realize and implement this philosophy. Sales is obvious. Structure – the business must have a solid structure and a layout of who we are and what we are trying to accomplish. This would include a mission statement, goals and business plans. Systems – this is a mapping out of processes which help to automate the sales and give the individual team members clear and concise, step-by-step, direction for every facet of business. Staff – the people you hire is one of the most important decisions you will make. You must have the right person in the right position with the right mindset. This is invaluable.

What would you tell young or new agents?

If you want to be successful, you must have passion, drive, strive to educate yourself daily, and connect with a successful agent you can call mentor. It doesn't matter what company you work for and what bells and whistles they offer; without a mentor you are statistically likely to fail quickly.

Chapter 5
Christopher Lengquist

LEAD GENERATE OR DIE!

Christopher Lengquist
Team Leader, KWR, Diamond Partners, Inc.
Broker/Owner, Ad Astra Realty, Inc.

Describe your business.

I am fortunate to have two roles; I am the owner/operator of Ad Astra Realty, Inc., a property management brokerage located in Olathe, Kansas. Additionally, I am the Team Leader of Keller Williams Realty, Diamond Partners, Inc. also located in Olathe.

My specialty as a real estate agent since 2002 was working with real estate investors, both neophyte and well-experienced, to evaluate, acquire, rehab and hold real estate investment properties. Through the years we added the specialty of managing said investment properties and through word of mouth have grown that portion of the business to be a rather sizeable concern in the Kansas City area.

Because of the unique experiences I've had in real estate over the years from struggling agent to agent to successful agent to brokerage owner to property manager to team leader, I have insights in to what works and doesn't work for the bell curve of licensees. To that point, I have launched a new endeavor, Realtepreneur.com.

Realtepreneur.com focuses on the four lanes an agent needs to conquer in order to have a big business and lead a big life.

i.   Database
ii. Time Management
iii. Money Management
iv. Team Building

This book is an excellent start to those wanting to learn more about their database and lead generation. The two go hand in hand.
What unique ways do you use to obtain leads?

Any dream worth having is worth setting aside lead generation time every workday, whether that is an hour a day, two hours a day or more. You MUST lead generate on a consistent basis. This is a time management issue as well as a lead generation must. Is that time spent on phone calls or blogging or handwritten cards? Well, maybe it is a mix of all those things, but if you set aside a minimum of two hours a day, every workday, for lead generation you will create business.

Diving a bit deeper here, I have found that most successful real estate agents get a preponderance of their leads through just two or three lead sources. For some, it may be referrals and farming, while for others it may be blogging and networking events, while still others may experience most of their success through cold calling expired listings and for sale by owners. The point is not what others are doing to lead generate, rather it's finding what you are good at doing.

There are over 25 identifiable lead generation strategies that successful agents use on a regular basis. Any one agent tends to try a great many of those methods before discovering their gifts and concentrating on those two to three lanes of leads. The big mistake most successful real estate agents make is that when they decide it is time to grow, they expand their lead generation rather than dig deeper into the methods with which they are already experiencing success. Rather than throw a couple thousand dollars at a new, untried method, I would advise an agent to break down where their last 100 closings came from. I promise you, there is a pattern in those closings that will jump off the page.

Once the pattern of closings is in front of you, there should be a firm resolve to dig deeper into that which has proven profitable in the past.   With a more mindful effort and renewed enthusiasm that which has been the best will almost assuredly lead to new heights.

When did you get into business?

May 2002

What is your WHY? Why did you get into the business?

I started real estate because I wanted control of my time and income. Deep down in my bones I always knew I was a bit of a serial entrepreneur, as are most real estate agents. I didn't perform well in college and I had always had a hard time working for others. Control was an issue, as was pride. On the other hand, I was never afraid of hard work nor did I lack creativity. Those are two traits which I am still proud of today.

Mentors and real estate heroes began to influence me. By the time I started my real estate career, I was thirty, seven years old. It was time to get serious about my life, and so I was determined to not flunk out of real estate. I had to provide for my family. I had to make this work.

My Big WHY

To create opportunity through the changing of mindsets such that I maximize peoples' vision, thoughts, income and opportunity so that they change their lives, the lives of their loved ones and charges from one generation to the next.

Today My BIG WHY is posted on the door of my office for all to see and a reminder to me each time I enter and leave.

What is your daily regimen that helps produce or maximize results you are seeking?

The two most important activities time-blocked on my calendar are for lead generation and self-improvement through reading, watching videos, meeting with my coach and attending educational opportunities.

The first note to take from my priorities is that I time-block them. They are that important. On my calendar I literally have those activities blocked as much as a year out. Sure, I leave room to move things around from time to time and to add more recent opportunities. However, I don't erase my lead generation time. If there is a conflict that cannot be avoided then I must rearrange my lead gen time rather than simply dismiss it. I must lead generate a minimum of 10 hours a week. Notice I used the word minimum. Closer to 15 would be so much better.

Secondly, you are never wasting your time educating and improving yourself. Many of you reading this will ask, "Chris, how can I sell more real estate than ever before and yet spend less time on the task? I mean, you have me spending 25% of my week lead generating and another 25 days a year training. How am I supposed to do all of this?" My answer? You just will. Why? Because you will be better prepared in mindset, discipline and you will have new- found knowledge in how to get more work done in less time. You will begin to learn that you don't need to be everything you've been to get to where you are going. Rather, you will learn to leverage time and people in a manner that allows more productivity in less time.

I promise. I've been there.

What do you do better than your competition?

At Ad Astra Realty Property Management here in Kansas City, we spend more time working on our business than in our business. Thank you to Michael Gerber, who wrote The E-myth, for his contribution to our business. Because of that we are constantly developing and refining systems that allow us to react quickly to the demands of our tenants and owners. These same systems and models allow our employees to have a better quality of life than those of our competitors.

Additionally, when our staff is working, they are more efficient and when they have time off they can enjoy what they are doing without having to worry about what is left undone at the workplace. This, of course, leads to better employees, and therefore happier customers.

How many transactions have you completed so far?

As of this writing, Ad Astra Realty Property Management manages 350 residential investment property units.
As a licensed real estate agent, I still get many leads off my database even though I do not actively engage in real estate sales any longer. But you know what is great? I will still cash 23 or more referral checks this year because I am happy to put people in contact with the right agent for them.

Think about the hardest thing you faced in business. How did or do you survive or get through tough times?

It takes mental toughness to survive and thrive in real estate sales and property management. More than any other trait that I see in successful real estate agents is simply the refusal to give in and give up. That is mental toughness.

I will never forget my early days in real estate. By that I mean both times. And by that I mean that I started my real estate career in Tulsa, OK in 2002, built a business I was proud of in just 26 months and then decided to move back to Kansas City in the fall of 2004. That meant starting all over again. And when the year 2009 arrived it was painful for everyone in real estate; I don't care who you were. Kansas City was shielded from the worst of the worst of the Great Recession, but nevertheless my income dropped by 31% from 2008 to 2009. (Here in KC the real estate recession really didn't get started till the fall of 2008, when the banks stopped lending.) Like many agents, I spent the first six months of the recession trying to decide if I was still in or out.

Each day I would wake up, do a little lead generating, write a blog post and then check the want ads! I won't get into the details, but I also took the time to open another business that would take a bit of time to make profitable. So here I was burning the candle at both ends and the fuel was what little money I had left.

And yet, the lead generation paid off. Someone in California read my Kansas City Real Estate Investing blog (BBQCapital.com) and gave me a call. Turned out they represented a fund that wanted to spend $5M in Kansas City and then have me manage the properties as well. That phone conversation turned it around for me.

That lead and subsequent business gave me the funding I needed to keep going and the affirmation that my lead generating was still out there and still working. You need to know that no matter what else I was doing to earn or find income, I never stopped lead generating.

LEAD GENERATE OR DIE!

Chapter 6
Carletha Frazier Singleton

LEAD GENERATE OR DIE!

Carletha Frazier Singleton
Carletha Marie & Associates at EXP Realty

Describe your business.

I am a licensed Real Estate Broker in South Carolina & Georgia. I recently sold my property management business, through which I once managed over 85 rental properties, to focus on Real Estate sales. The majority of my Real Estate sales business comes from online leads.

What unique ways do you use to obtain leads?

Leads within my business are primarily obtained from online marketing. Whether it be blogs or social media with target marketing. Any offline marketing that is done usually directs individuals back online with some type of call to action or offer for an e-book or home value analysis.

When did you get into business?

I was introduced to the real estate industry in 2004 as a leasing consultant within apartment communities. Then I obtained my real estate sales license in 2005 and later obtained my broker's license and opened a brokerage in 2009.

What is your WHY? Why did you get into the business?

When I first got into the business it was mainly to be my own boss, to be in control of my time along with the unlimited income potential. Today, that reason has changed just a bit as I have grown a strong passion to help people in addition to being able to spend time with my children.

What is the thing that motivates you? What drives you?

My motivation is really to not be average and avoid fitting in with the crowd. To maintain a successful business and not miss a beat far as my kids are concerned. My drive would be to be able to show other young women, whether single or married, that there are no limits other than the ones set by oneself. And of course I want to be someone my sons can look up to and understand that all things are possible.

What is your daily regimen that helps produce or maximize results you are seeking?

Daily lead generating for me is basically creating content that people are looking for within a blog or social media post and then following up with leads that have been generated previously.

What do you do better than your competition?

Online Marketing. I'm able to market properties that reach Google to attract more leads. Not many other agents understand how to market a home other than placing it in the MLS. So with landing pages, blogging and other marketing techniques, that would be my strength.

How many transactions have you completed so far?

I have completed 62 transactions after going full time in sales in 2014 after running my property management business of 85 rental units.

What is your volume of transactions so far?

Total volume is $10.1 million

Think about the hardest thing you faced in business/life. How did or do you survive or get through tough times?

The hardest thing that I have faced is not having buyers or sellers to speak with due to working in my business rather than working on my business. Lead generation is the solution to that problem. Developing discipline to lead gen every day can be tough, however. Time blocking and having a productivity checklist is key.

What would you tell your younger self?

I would tell my younger self to remove all limits and fail forward fast. Find a mentor who is willing to pour into you and help with the full understanding of this business. Personal development is a must.

What would you tell young or new agents?

I would tell new agents to understand that this is a business and it should be treated as such under the fundamentals of running a real estate business. Go out and get the information you need to succeed and ask lots of questions. Again, a mentor or coach are key. Don't wait on your Broker, you are in business for yourself.

Chapter 7
J. René Ward

J. René Ward
The Best Agents In Texas

Describe your business.

Best Agents in Texas is a full-service real estate company that provides buying, selling, leasing and investments services to its clients in Austin, TX and surrounding communities.

Austin is a great city, with a wide variety of homes; the Capital City provides its homeowners with a balance of a strong economy, good education, attractive housing, a relatively pleasant climate, and plenty of things to do. Home construction is still going strong and builders are offering high-end features and numerous amenities. Many of Austin's luxury homes also boast amazing views of downtown skylines, lakes, golf courses or hill country and some have private gated entrances. From new construction to waterfront homes to large condos with panoramic views, Austin offers a wide variety of home options to explore.

What unique ways do you use to obtain leads?

I try not to be a secret agent. I work hard at getting out there and networking. For me this is not my natural state, but I know the importance of relationships.

I teach real estate classes at the local real estate schools, boards, associations and offer classes at my office. I also take classes outside of my local geographic area and outside of my current market. For example, in the last 30 days I have gone to Galveston, TX to take luxury classes because I want to do more luxury real estate. I extend my reach by getting with people who do what I would like to do. People tend to be more generous with people out of their market area; you're not seen as the competition. Traveling nationally also allows me to know different real estate markets and establish relationships for future referrals.

I have written several books that broaden my brand and allows me to share my ideas with others. Being an author also does a few other things: It makes me the perceived "expert" in a subject matter, gives me credibility with potential clients, I can generate more leads, close more deals, charge higher fees, and get better speaking engagements - it's the new business card.

Lastly, I buy help. When there is more to do than there is time, I hire a virtual assistant. The assistant saves me time, money and frustration. In Gary Keller's book, The One Thing, he asks - What's the ONE Thing you can do such that by doing it everything else will be easier or unnecessary? Often my one thing is to hire great help so that I can be with clients, teach and speak to a larger audience.

Don't be a secret agent! Get out there and network. Leverage your time well.

When did you get into business?

I got into the real estate business in 2002. I started my brokerage in 2004. Prior to real estate I held management positions in several high-tech companies. IBM for 19 years, Toshiba for a few years and then Dell Computers for a few years. After that, I joined a startup, that didn't really start up. They laid off the entire marketing team for which I was the Vice President.

I decided to become a real estate agent after exploring my next job offer in San José, CA. I realized I would have to leave my custom-built home in Texas and change my lifestyle a lot, to afford California real estate. That's when I made a list of pros and cons for the next chapter in my life. I bought my first home when I was 22. I had lived in 13 states and bought and sold about 30 houses. I loved relocating and buying new homes. Real estate seemed to be a natural fit. It was the right choice for me and I still enjoy what I do.

What is your WHY? Why did you get into the business?

Real estate makes a dramatic difference in the lives of people. This component was missing from my corporate career. I enjoyed my marketing positions in high tech and all the benefits that went along with it, but honestly, I wasn't making a difference in the lives of others. In real estate, I see the difference owning a home makes in families and communities. It impacts the financial health and wealth in our community for generations. I still get great pleasure and personal satisfaction when helping a first-time home buyer.

What is the thing that motivates you? What drives you?

What motivates me is giving back - mentoring, coaching and training. I have been blessed and my passion is to pass it on. The word itself pass-it-on expresses my motivation. How do I pass on what I know before I go? I want to help people grow and make this profession better. I am not going to do this forever, but the ability to leave my impact by passing my knowledge and experience along is important to me. We can begin to change how people look at this profession.

What is your daily regimen that helps produce or maximize results you are seeking?

My daily regiment varies. I make it a point to start the day with quiet time. It centers me. I try to keep a To Do list, but having an assistant helps me to prioritize and organize. I travel every month but I try not to be out of the office more than a few consecutive days. I work mostly with sellers and do listing appointments, agreements and negotiations; which gives me some flexibility. Technology keeps me accessible to my team and clients. I am in the office at least 3 days per week. As a team, we lead generate every day! I pay a company to do outbound calls into our farm areas and to nurture the leads. They set appointments and we show up and hopefully close the deal.

What do you do better than your competition?

We customize service to the individual. I often say we give great customer service but it may not look the same to each customer because it is really customized for that specific individual's need. We are a small team with a strong referral business because we pay attention to the small stuff. People remember how you made them feel. It's that feeling that generates referrals.

How many transactions have you completed so far?

Best Agents in Texas has completed over 1,000 transactions, about 100 per year. I created the brokerage in 2004. Our average home sale price is $235,000. I have 4 agents and an office manager.

What is your volume vs. your # of transactions so far?

For listings, we get 90% of the listings we go on. As for buyers, the rate isn't quite that high. We get 75% of the buyers we encounter and interact with. That percentage is lower mainly because most are not ready to buy. Sometimes they don't realize they are not ready until they have had a conversation with us. It is more important to me that they stay in their home, not just purchase a home. So, our buyer conversion rate has always been lower than our listing conversion rate.

Think about the hardest thing you faced in business. How did or do you survive or get through tough times?

Sometimes the hardest thing in business is staying in business. Keeping your offerings, your skills and your services fresh and up-to-date. Reinventing your model while staying true to your core principles. There is always a struggle between the bright, new, shining object and sustaining your people skills. Real estate is still a relationship business. People will always be the consistent denominator. Technology will never replace good people skills. Yet, we are in front of a screen for a large part of the day. I challenge you to have more face to face interactions and watch what happens to your business. There is always balance. I don't dwell on the struggle. The struggle is only there to make us stronger!

What would you tell young or new agents?

Don't forget why you became a Realtor. If you forget that we are servants, here to provide service to people who need our help. If you forget that we are doing missionary work that has a larger impact on our community. If you forget that it's NOT all about the money and it IS all about the relationship. If you can remember that this is your assignment, your purpose, your time, then the transaction is easy. We are helping people solve problems.

In my community, there are over 15,000 other agents the customer could be sitting in the presence of, but there is a reason this person is in front of me. Don't miss the opportunity to make a difference.

J. René welcomes your questions and feedback. Feel free to contact her using the contact information below:

For real estate:

Best Agents in Texas
10435 Burnet Road #107 Austin, TX
78758 512.388.3313
www.BestAgentsInTexas.comAgent@Best
AgentsInTexas.com

For speaking engagements:

www.JReneSpeaks.com
888.TX Agent (892-4368)

Chapter 8
Roz Bazile

Roz Bazile
Wealth Advisory Group

Describe your business.

We offer financial consulting to help clients reach their personal and business goals. Some of the tools we use are training, workshops, strategic planning, bookkeeping, tax preparation and more.

What unique ways do you use to obtain leads?

I've partnered with someone who is Hispanic and bilingual in order to reach and serve the Hispanic community, which is the largest minority group in Texas. Because of the language barrier and lack of training in money management many of them have been taken advantage of by unscrupulous business owners or scammers. Our goal is to make it right so we also joined a Hispanic Chamber to build relationships with business owners to help them not just stay in business but grow their business so they can go back to their employees and community to pass down the knowledge they gain.

When did you get into business?

I started my first business in 2000 doing taxes and accounting out of my home, and eventually opened a storefront location. I have since relocated, revamped my business model and relaunched in 2014.

What is your WHY for launching your business?

When I first started business, it was to have flexibility so I could be available for my two children who were only 11 and 8 at the time. When I relaunched, it was from a deep desire to help people achieve their financial goals since I had made many mistakes myself and learned so much over the years.

What is the thing that motivates you? What drives you?

At the core it is really helping other people succeed. For a lot of people it's their kids. I love my kids and want them to succeed, but I realized I want others to succeed too. It doesn't matter where they are or where they've been. I genuinely get excited for others' success, and especially those who have the odds against them.

What is your daily regimen that helps produce or maximize results you are seeking?

Staying connected on social media but also doing something every day that moves me one step closer to my goals no matter how small.

What do you do better than your competition or other businesses like yours?

I connect on a personal level so I can see the bigger picture to help clients become successful. I don't just do taxes. I ask questions so that I know what tax advice to give that might have an effect on their financial goals or ability to build wealth, for example.

Think about the hardest thing you faced in business. How did or do you survive or get through tough times?

The hardest thing was relaunching with a full-time job, so time management was an issue. I had to bring a team on board to help, which was new for me because when I first started I did not have a job so I was able to devote all my time to my business. I get through any tough time by taking time out to put things in perspective, reevaluating my goals, and moving forward.

What would you tell your younger self?

I would tell my younger self that your opportunities are greater than what you see. Don't be afraid to explore your options. You will make mistakes and it will be OK. Don't let fear rob you of living your dreams. Do it afraid. Your future self will thank you.

What would you tell young or new agents?

I would tell them that while you are making your clients' dreams come true, don't forget about your own. You have the greatest opportunity to build a solid foundation to build wealth for yourself and for generations to come. Connect with a business coach or experienced agent to develop a plan for your success. Success comes in phases. Be prepared, be consistent and be flexible.

Chapter 9
John Mayfield

John Mayfield
The Business Tech Guy

Describe your business.

I am a real estate broker in my 38th year, and also provide speaking, training and other educational opportunities to real estate professionals. My real estate business model at this time focuses on a virtual office concept. I would consider myself a small boutique agency.

What unique ways do you use to obtain leads?

My primary focus for developing leads is through my sphere of influence. Although I do prospect for new business through farming neighborhoods, calling on for sale by owners and utilizing an expired listing program, my primary source of business (70%) from the last two years has been through my past clients, customers and referrals, and recommendations from this group.

When did you get into the business?

As noted earlier, I obtained my real estate license in 1978 at the age of 18. I do hold broker's licenses in Missouri and Florida.

What is your WHY?

Why did you get into the business? I got into real estate by accident. My mother had informed me that the minimum age requirement had recently changed in Missouri to the age of 18 for applying for a real estate license. Believe it or not, I turned 18 in May, and by June I was licensed as a real estate salesperson in Missouri. Since my mother had a real estate office, I thought it would be a good idea for me to get my license and to help her with her agency. I had been working for my father and his retail store since the age of 16 selling men's clothing, so my background in sales was somewhat proficient, and I thought that it only made sense for me to help my mother with her real estate organization.

What is the thing that motivates you?

I believe what motivates me the most is when I can set goals and have a vision for accomplishments I want to achieve. I think having a lot of activities and tasks on my daily to-do's is also a motivator. When I was a senior in college I was forced to take 19 hours my last semester to graduate with my class in May. That semester was my highest grade point average in college. I've continued that same philosophy in my business life and have noticed that when I do not have a lot of things or tasks on my calendar, my productivity tends to decrease. So for me, the why and what motivates me is having a lot of things and items to achieve and putting those goals and objectives in writing so that I can formulate a vision for my future.

What is your daily regimen that helps produce or maximize results you are seeking?

It is writing down my goals each and every day. I have a list that I will add daily tasks to and I highlight and check out those items once they are completed. I also have a list of goals that I continually look at in my Evernote account to help keep me on track and motivate me to achieve my goals.

What do you do better than your competition?

I believe what helps me beat the competition is providing more value added services to my clients and customers. I'm good at technology, and I know a lot about marketing, but I also realize that if I can prove to the client or customer that I'm going to bring more value to the table for them than my competition, they will want to do business with me over my competitors.

How many transactions have you completed so far?

Currently, I do anywhere between 10 to 20 real estate transactions per year. However, the bulk of my business is through speaking, writing and consulting with other real estate organizations. I have personally been involved with thousands of transactions over my lifetime, and I continue to do the minimum number of transactions to be included with the annual awards program thrown by our local board of Realtors. Again, most of my business is generated through past clients, customer's and referrals.

What is your volume vs. your # of transactions so far?

My volume ranges around the $2 million mark. The average sales price in my area is right at $100,000.

Think about the hardest thing you faced in business. How did or do you survive or get through tough times?

For me, the most challenging time was after I sold my real estate company in 2006 and went to work for a bank. Within a short period, I was unemployed had signed a noncompete clause and was also in the midst of a terrible real estate downturn. Even through all of those challenges, I formulated a budget and knew exactly what I needed to achieve each and every month to break even and make a profit. Through that, I was able to formulate a game plan and learn how to produce multiple streams of income to weather the storm. I also learned during those challenges and trials that it was important for me to stay focused by reading positive books, listening to motivational tapes and hanging around the right people who could continue to give me the optimistic and positive attitude I needed to survive.

What would you tell your younger self?

Don't ever give up on your dreams, anything is possible! Spend more time reading and investing in education and find out what your passion is and then make that your work.

What would you tell young or new agents?

Invest in education, develop an excellent list of your raving fans, a sphere of influence, or people you know and would like to do business with. These are the individuals who can help you grow your real estate business. Try to find an article or something you can read each and every day to learn a little bit more about the profession. Dress professionally and hang around with the right people. As I stated in the last question, make sure that you're following what your passion is! I love what I do, and I've even figured out new things that I have a greater passion for, and because of that, I can invest countless hours of time enjoying what I'm doing and pursuing the opportunity to add value and help other people.

ABOUT THE AUTHORS

Dr. Tameka Bryant

Dr. Tameka Bryant is President of Think Realty Real Estate Services with operations in 8 states. She is also a multi-state licensed broker and a certified instructor with the National Association of Realtors.

Dr. Bryant started her full time real estate career in 2004 when she started The Real Estate House in Kansas City. Her first national account was with Freddie Mac and she quickly became a Master Listing Broker. After achieving Realtor of the Year, Dr. Bryant became the first African American President of the Multiple Listing Service.

Dr. Bryant has closed more than 2,000 real estate transactions and maintains successful businesses including two real estate schools and projects working with developers, investors, and agents.

Dr. Bryant works diligently to promote home ownership daily. Growing up in the Bronx, Tameka's parents didn't own their home and were lifetime renters. She made a promise to herself that she would one day own her home and provide her children with the opportunities not afforded to her. She did more than that. She made it her life's work to help others understand the importance of owning their home and building wealth.

Over the years, along with her service, Tameka has been a member of the following organizations: American Business Women's Association, Kansas Association of Realtors, National Association of Women Business Owners, Greater

Kansas City and Olathe Chamber of Commerce and Wor in Public Policy to name a few.

Dr. Bryant has been featured in several publications incluc Black Enterprise and has published books on Amazon, Bar & Noble and Kindle. She is an educator and has a real pass for educating young adults. Since her first day, as an adju professor in New York, she has never given up her passio teach others and make a real difference.

In addition to her managing her real estate businesses, s continues to invest herself. With properties in 5 states s stays on the go and stays ready for the next opportunity. an investor herself, she understands what it takes to maint and develop productive portfolios and is passionate abc helping others do the same.

Tameka is married to Jeffrey and has two children, Kiane a Kyle.

Jessica Hensley

Jessica Hensley, Age 32- Broker/Owner of Heritage Hom Realty Coffeyville, Kansas and Independence, Kansas. S has been licensed since 2003 in Oklahoma and in Kan since2005.

Jessica opened Heritage Homes Realty in Coffeyville January, 2015, with one other agent. 2016 brought lots changes, with the addition of eight agents and one n location in Independence.

From 2003 through 2014, she was a part-time agent, wh working as a Financial Advisor and an Insurance Agent. 2015, she was the number one residential agent in her M with 63 transactions and $6,597,100. In 2016, she added agents to her team and doubled production to 1 transactions and $12,660,020 in sales!

Jessica has been married to Cody Hensley since 2004, th met in Stillwater, Oklahoma, while attending OSU. They ha one son, Henry, who is 4, and the light of their lives!

LEAD GENERATE OR DIE!

Trisha Alton

Trisha Alton epitomizes integrity, energy, hard work a creative service in every detail of real estate transactio Trisha grew up in Weston, Missouri, and started her sa habit at the age of 16, selling sandwiches and ice cream a local eatery. She has continued building a successful car and team in real estate for over 12 years in the Kansas C KS & MO metro area. She has worked every aspect of t industry representing sellers, buyers, investors and banks the residential market. Trisha also owns a prope management company where she manages and owns her o rentals, and she also flips homes on the side.

Trisha is married to Jared Alton, and they have a daugh named Chloe and three dogs. After selling a client a ho and attending a BBQ as a thank you, Trisha met Jared a later the two started dating. In November 2014, they g married. And since, Jared has adopted Chloe as his ov Trisha enjoys spending free time with her family and going vacations to experience other areas.

Trisha has been trained and inspired in sales by some of t best from Tom Ferry Coaching to Kansas City's own Tame Bryant, who is a business owner, educator and author. Tris uses her experience and foresight to proactively addre details before they become a problem. She and her team wo with clients to initiate communication in every detail of t transaction, from the first phone call all the way to close. S leads, trains and motivates her team to communicate w clients better than none. Five words you can count on fre Trisha Alton; love, integrity, commitment, passion and fun.

James Like

James Like is a multi-million-dollar real estate sales producer. He is the founder and broker for Revolution Real Estate in Burleson, Texas. He has been in real estate as a salesman since 2006 and an investor since 2000. James manages a team of professionals and admin staff as well as multiple other businesses including property management, investing and real estate coaching. He is passionate about missions and outreach and has a goal of reaching thousands of people by establishing micro-businesses in various countries of the world.

James is married to Jessi and they have three daughters, Jayden, Jazzlyn and Juliana. They all enjoy world travel but are rooted in Burleson.

Christopher Lengquist

Chris Lengquist is the Broker/Owner of Ad Astra Realty, Inc., a property management firm operating in and around Kansas City, MO as well as the Team Leader of Keller Williams Realty, Diamond Partners, Inc. located in Olathe Kansas. Chris is also the energy behindRealtepreneur.com.

Chris started his real estate career in Tulsa, OK in the spring of 2002 and moved his real estate career to his hometown of Kansas City, on the Kansas side, in 2004. His career has been marked by excitement and frustration as well as victory and defeat. With each defeat came opportunity to learn, adapt and to rise again.

Finding that owning a real estate career wasn't much different from the other businesses Chris has been involved with and/or owned, his mission has become to educate real estate agents across America as to where their focus should be in order to have a big business and a big life.

LEAD GENERATE OR DIE!

Carletha Frazier Singleton

Carletha Singleton is a Licensed Real Estate Broker in 2 states with over 10 years of experience in the Real Estate Industry.

Carletha started mentoring and coaching business individuals and entrepreneurs about 5 years ago and her passion to empower others continues to grow. She is a certified mentor for EXP Realty where she helps guide both new and seasoned agents with their Real Estate Business. Her enthusiasm for technology & passion lead her to become a certified trainer for the National Association of Realtors.

J. René Ward

Broker and owner of Best Agents in Texas, J. René Ward strives to provide each and every client with an experience that is worthy of referrals. Best Agents in Texas is a full-service real estate company that provides buying, selling leasing and investments services to its clients in Austin and surrounding communities.

Austin is a great city with a variety of many luxury homes; the Capital City provides its owners with privacy, high-end features and numerous amenities. Many of Austin's luxury homes also boast amazing views of downtown skylines, lakes golf courses or hill country and some have private gated entrances. From new construction to waterfront homes t large condos with panoramic views, Austin offers a wide variety of luxury home options to explore.

J. René is an expert in her market. She is the past President of the Austin Association of Real Estate Brokers and currently serves on the Board of Directors for the National Association of Real Estate Brokers. She is an instructor for the National Association of REALTORS®, Texas Association of REALTORS® Texas Real Estate Commission and several real estate boards. She was formerly the President of the Williamson County Association of REALTORS® and has received a number of awards including REALTOR® of the Year. J. René recently has won the TAR Educator of the Year and the Platinum Top 50 Realtor Award. J René was also selected by the Women's Council of REALTORS® "Businesswoman of the Year." J. René has appeared on Home and Garden TV's "House Hunters" and has authored "The Ultimate Real Estate Agent" and "The Listing Guide"

To date, she has also sold the most expensive home in Round Rock, TX.

As an individual who values education, J. René holds a MBA from Nova University and several real estate designations (ABR, CNE, CRB, CREI, GRI, CRS, ePRO, PMN, PIC, SRES, TRLP & TAHS) allowing her to serve her clients with experience and expert advice.

Prior to her work as a Realtist®/ REALTOR®, J. René was a marketing executive for IBM, Toshiba America, Dell Computers and other high tech companies. J. René has moved over 15 times, raised in Philadelphia, Pennsylvania, before settling down in Round Rock, Texas in1998.

Roz Bazile

Roz Bazile knows the challenges of getting your business and personal financial house in order. After a devastating divorce she found herself starting over from scratch and had to rebuild her life and finances. As a result, she is highly motivated to help others build a solid financial foundation.

Roz has a B.S. in Management/Accounting with over 20 years of experience as the Controller of multi-million dollar corporations in various industries. She now uses her expertise to help small business owners and upcoming entrepreneurs make their dreams a reality. She is a licensed real estate agent, life insurance agent, investor, and business coach. Roz enjoys traveling, reading and spending time with family and friends.

You can contact Roz at:
www.BuildingWealthAdvisoryGroup.com.

John Mayfield

John Mayfield received his real estate license in 1978 at the age of 18. John has been a practicing broker since 1981 and has owned and operated three offices in Southeast Missouri. John has taught pre and post license real estate courses since 1988. John has earned the ABR®, ABRM, CRB, CIPS, e PRO®, GRI and SRS designations throughout his real estate tenure. John is also a 2015 Graduate from REALTOR® University's Masters of Real Estate Program, and recipient o the Capstone Award for his thesis paper. John has earned both REALTOR-Associate and REALTOR of the Year from his local board and received the 2014 Richard A. Mendenha Leadership award from the state of Missouri.

John is a Senior GRI instructor for The Missouri Associatio of REALTORS® and the Arkansas Association c REALTORS® and teaches for the REBI, Real Esta Business Institute.

John has spoken to thousands of real estate professiona throughout his tenure. He has been a featured speaker at th National Association of REALTORS® conventions c several occasions and taught in the Technology Resour Center for NAR. He is the author of eight books and creat of the "5-Minutes Series for Real Estate Agents," Cenga Learning, with over 25,000 copies sold. He is the co-author 21 Mistakes Real Estate Brokers Make and How to Avo Them, Acclaim Press.

John has served as a contributing editor to REALTOR Magazine Online, and a real estate consultant and influenc for Hewlett Packard. John is also active on a local, state ar

ional level for the REALTORS® Association, and served
the 2010 President of the CRB Council of Real Estate
okers and Managers. John has recently become an active
iner assisting European real estate brokers and managers
1 spends part of the year living in France, involved with
ernational property relations.

an has two children, Alyx and Anne, and he and his wife
rry live in Farmington, MO, where John owns and
erates a "virtual" real estate firm and speaks on a full-time
iis.

NOTES

NOTES

62923676R00060

Made in the USA
Lexington, KY
21 April 2017